The Productive Woman

The Ultimate Guide to Getting Things Done and Increasing Productivity for Women

Janet R. Lee

All Rights Reserved. No part of this publication may be reproduced in any form or by any means, including scanning, photocopying, or otherwise without prior written permission of the copyright holder. Copyright © 2014

Table of Contents

PRODUCTIVITY – UNDERSTANDING THE MAGIC WORD 5
- What is Productivity? 5
- Why Is Productivity Important? 7
- Can You Measure Productivity? 8

WOMEN AND PRODUCTIVITY – THE UNACKNOWLEDGED STORIES 11
- Workplace 12
  - *A Sign of Changing Times* 13
- Home and the Community 14
- Are Women Less Productive Than Men? 15

WOMEN PRODUCTIVITY – WHAT DO THE STUDIES SAY? 17
- Women Work Harder than Men in Workplaces 17
- Working Flexible Hours Increase Productivity in Women 18
- Businesses with Women Do Better 19

IMPROVING WOMEN'S PRODUCTIVITY – LEARNING THE TRICKS OF THE TRADE 21
- Do the Hardest Task of the Day First 21
- Don't be Afraid to Seek Help 21
- Delegate Your Work 21
- Eliminate Distractions 21
- Reward Yourself 22
- Take Notes all the Time 22
- Make a Checklist 22

PRODUCTIVITY SECRETS FROM ACCOMPLISHED WOMEN 23
- Make Time for Down Time 23

Take the Bull By the Horns...23
Don't Multi-Task 23
Cut Down on Social Media 24
Giving the Right Environment..24
CONCLUSION...25

PRODUCTIVITY – UNDERSTANDING THE MAGIC WORD

It's a fact that we all want to perform our best, whether it's in our professional or personal life. In order to deliver our best, we need to be productive, and that requires a lot of work. On the other hand, before we start talking about how you can become productive, it is important to understand what productivity actually is.

While you might find different perceptions about what productivity is, knowing the actual definition is where you should start. Once you know what productivity is, you can move on to understand why it matters to be productive, and how you can achieve productivity in every aspect of your life.

What is Productivity?

In simple words, productivity is the best and easiest ways of using all the resources that are at hand (even if it is a simple thing like pen and paper, you use them in the best way possible) in order to get the best output. You go, girl!

These resources can include a wide variety of objects like the materials, space, energy, equipment, finance, information, knowledge, people and time around you. When you are using them, try to use them to best of their advantage but in a manner which doesn't make them clash against each other.

For the best way to manage the resources that you have at hand, you need to understand a few things.

First of all, you need to have a clear understanding of what you need to do to get the result you are looking for. If the paperwork needs to be filed first, do it. If the dishes need to be done before you can relax, do it. Follow Nike's motto and *'just do it'*.

After understanding this factor, you need to create a game plan which identifies all the different tasks that you have to complete before you can achieve your final goal.

Next step, you need to think about the path that you want to take in order to complete all these tasks you just outlined. Think of this step like creating a road map for yourself in order to find the buried treasure. X marks the spot. Don't take it like a Snakes and Ladder game board; going where the dice throw leads. Because in real life, when you do go down a snake, the next ladder isn't always a dice throw away.

When you're creating your roadmap, be sure to assign a time limit to each task, like you would if you had to stop at a pit stop on your travels. This will allow you to create set a time limit for the work to be done in. It will definitely stop you from getting tempted to dawdle and delay doing it.

Determine what kind of resources you will need to complete all the tasks that you have, within your assigned time period. Now that you have identified the X where the treasure is buried, you will need the proper tools to dig it out. You won't go digging for treasure with a spoon in your pocket so be sure that you have your spade and pick axe with you in order to ease up the process of digging.

Once all the equipment you need have been collected, make sure to begin right away. Keep a check of the progress that you have made by marking each activity as a milestone that you have to overcome. Check where there might be obstacles which could slow down your progress. If you do spot such disruptions, don't get worried. Simply make a few editions to your action plan and fix the problem.

While it is popularly believed that the two key principles on which the concept of productivity is based are time and motion, you should know that these principles are not the true representatives of what the concept of productivity stands for.

Time and motion are simple aspects but they are, at all times, within the hand of individual workers. Productivity is more concerned with the planning portion of the job. In such situations the main goal of reading the productivity of the job is based on the whole outcome and not how different resources in the plan would be used individually.

Why Is Productivity Important?

Now that we have identified productivity, let's see why it is important for women in every wake of their life, whether they are carrying out a personal task or a professional assignment. For us, especially our girls who are working; we'll often find that we are short of time to complete our tasks and manage our professional and household responsibilities. It can get extremely frustrating when that happens.

Sometimes, it is extremely difficult to maintain a balance between our personal and professional roles. A business woman by day, a mum by night, there aren't many people who have such an existence other than superheroes but Marvel and DC are definitely not looking around for Super Mum. Nonetheless, when you're feeling the pressure in this scenario, this is where the concept of productivity can bring a huge improvement in your life.

Nowadays, most of your time is wasted because you haven't planned things beforehand. This can instantly spiral out of control with Mr. Indecision taking the lead and confusing you about how and what to do next. The largest result is more wasted time than anything else.

On the other hand, if you start your day by planning, you will know exactly what needs to be done, what you need to accomplish that task and how quickly you can get it done. This way, you will be able to finish more work in the given time and you will be more productive.

Can You Measure Productivity?

It is always possible to measure your own personal productivity but it isn't always the easiest thing to keep track of. This is mainly because it's often subjective.

Nonetheless, there are ways through which you can record your personal productivity on any day. The most commonly used way to measure personal productivity is to keep track of your downtime activities in a day. Here is what you need to do:

Make a list of all your daily activities, including your downtime tasks such as watching television, surfing the Internet, reading books etc.

Start taking note of the time you spend every day in these downtime activities aka the time you spend 'not working'. Yeah, you heard us, quit slacking off.

Now, slowly, start cutting down the time you devote to these downtime activities. This doesn't mean that you stop doing these small hobbies that bring you joy, just be sure to set a strict limit on the time you spend on them. Don't let them hamper your productivity; use them as small rewards for yourself or a little downtime to blow off steam.

By regulating your breaks, you can use this extra time in your routine to finish a task that usually gets neglected, whether it's a household chore or a professional project.

Even little changes in your schedule here and there can add up to a lot and boost your productivity. Waking up a little earlier once in a while or sleeping a little bit later to finish a task that is being neglected for a long time can also help you increase your productivity.

If you want to learn about more ways to increase your productivity take a look at the other sections of this eBook. Once you are done with this eBook, we hope that you will know exactly how you can enhance your productivity and output in a manageable way.

WOMEN AND PRODUCTIVITY – THE UNACKNOWLEDGED STORIES

When it comes to productivity, it is a popular belief that you just happen to have a hands down lead over your male compatriots at home. Now this is a very traditional belief. Moreover, this often means that your actual levels of productivity, at work, are not being considered.

If you want an example of how unacknowledged these levels of productivity are, just take a look at the salary figures that men and women pull in from their respective jobs. At times, there is a huge difference between these numbers even if the positions are the same or higher. Now why is that?

While a lot of speculation can be raised about it, including the fact that women are being discriminated against, it's not all black and white when you take a closer look at it. Even though many people may want to take that path and put it down to the macho need to stand out above women, the question still remains; are women more or as productive as men?

If looked on from a general view, it does appear that women just happen to be much better planners, multi-taskers and can naturally identify what needs to be done immediately and what can be put on the back burner. You just have a better brain.

However, while we're all patting ourselves on the back and feeling proud, you have to realize that not all women are productive. It's not a widely known fact, but, some of us do slack off. Don't tell anyone. You are only human after all.

Most of the time, you have other responsibilities to consider as well and often times, you're just tired from looking after the home and making sure everything is fine.

On the other hand, we are often the un-sung heroes of the workforce. It's not a popular saying but it can be said that behind every successful organization is a room full of women fussing and fretting over what needs to be done. Actually, that's not a saying at all. We just made it up.

But if you are wondering about how exactly women are productive, let's take a closer look at a short history of women at work and home.

Workplace

Nowadays, without question, women are considered to be productive members of an organization. A team that is diverse is far more likely to succeed be more productive in everything they do. Think of it like being a woman pirate on a crew full of men. They don't really consider the fact that you're a woman as long as you help keep the ship afloat.

However, this was not always the case for women. I mean they weren't always considered productive. There have been actual pirate women in history.

Now back to productivity and the place of women in the workplace. During the 1990's they were in many ways limited to the role of a secretary. Since we are better planners, and can pay more attention to detail and everyone loves to hear a pleasant voice on the phone, it was unfortunate that for a very long time, they were confined to this role.

On a pirate boat, that's like being assigned deck scrubbing duty again and again.

A Sign of Changing Times

On the other hand, women managers were not unheard of. But they were still a rarity, like a white lion, to find in a largely male dominated world. Since everyone was so busy gaping at them in shock, their productivity could not exactly be measured.

Slowly over time, women have started to infiltrate to other management and high level positions owing to the fact that they can help boost productivity immensely.

Compared to our male counterparts, women managers did not exhibit enough masculine attributes such as task oriented directives. We definitely can't smoke cigars and knock back scotch tumblers like they do.

On the other hand, we had better ratings for utilizing non-masculine practices of leadership such as promoting participation and better interpersonal relationships.

Taking that fact into mind recent times also show that women in the workforce are better educated in comparison to men and exhibit more productive traits since masculine work practices are being outmoded.

With the new drift towards IT, many businesses rely on incorporating non-masculine problem solving and participative skills which women really shine in. We naturally know how to work with other people and make sure everyone gets along with each other. Sharing is caring and it means the mutual benefit of all, we don't hesitate to take that route.

As far as the work place is concerned, it really seems like we have got the productivity factor nailed down and show great progress in it.

Home and the Community

Now let's turn towards women in the home and the community. While the home is considered to the natural domain of women, it is wrong to expect that we will naturally know and understand what to do to improve productivity at home.

While some us are natural planners and know exactly how to manage our homes, some have had to learn this skill. However, no matter what kind of woman is looking after the home, their productivity has always mattered for the wellbeing of their family.

Overtime though the role in the world around us has expanded and many women now choose to work and look after their homes as well. We are multi talented and if working meant that we could gain equality, standing next to our husbands as the bread winners then that was something that almost every woman wanted to do.

As we have become more productive at work, our productivity and contribution at home and in the community have grown as well. With more economic stability, the overall wellbeing of our children has also improved.

Children who received better education opportunities, are also more likely to grow up and contribute to society in a positive manner.

As a whole, while people have complained that working women have a lesser role in their homes and in the community, which is a point for contention and can open up a whole other can of confusion, we, are productive members of our society, at home, work and in our communities as well.

Are Women Less Productive Than Men?

In the long run, this is something that will always pops rears up its ugly head every now and then. Are women more productive than men? A lot of us have really become fed up of this comparison to men. Just like men have their own merits and demerits, we have our own merits and demerits as well.

If you take a look at all the roles that a woman is expected to play such as be a housewife, a mother, a chef, a care giver, a manager in one single day, it can be supposed that we are more productive than men. On the other hand, there are men who are also full-filling these roles every day. Does that make them any less productive than us?

The best thing to look at when such an argument does show up is to understand that no human being, whether man or woman is perfect. Each has their own faults and qualities that make them stand out and it would be wrong to say which one is better.

We can be better at some things and fail at things too. Productive women are able to master and control everything around them but less productive women may find themselves stumbling to keep up. Similarly, productive men can be more efficient at home and at work as well while less productive men will also find problems in fulfilling their roles and duties at home and at work.

The main thing to keep in mind is that if you know how to be productive, it doesn't matter whether you are a man or a woman, it will show through in everything you do. Therefore, it is wrong to look at it solely from one point of view and get hung up about that.

Luckily, there have been official studies conducted about how productive we are in comparison to men and if you are interested, take a look at the next chapter where we will be covering a few studies that have actually been conducted on the productivity that women have.

WOMEN PRODUCTIVITY – WHAT DO THE STUDIES SAY?

Before you start frowning about why this topic was even studied, you should realize that productivity is a big thing. It's like the wind. You can't see it but you can definitely feel it when it's there.

Productivity around the house and workplace are extremely important but what you should keep in mind is the fact that men are automatically accepted as productive members of society. They're the bread winners and protectors and for many, many years they have had that role without any one saying it should be otherwise.

The main thing to keep in mind is the fact that these time held roles have begun to change. Women have started to help out at work and hold their own as well.

However, it is something which has always aroused the curiosity of many people. Among the many points that come up, the following are the most prominent ones

Women Work Harder than Men in Workplaces

Do women actually work harder at work? If you know how well you work, you will be liable to say *'Of course, I do!'* On the other hand, not everyone is able to answer with such confidence.

Everyone has their good days and bad days but luckily, you've got researchers on your side.

Research conducted by the Ponemon Institute in 2013, showcased the fact that the women were definitely more productive compared to the men who were there for the research.

The research was conducted by placing 274 men and women from different fields like consumer products, financial services, health care, energy etc in a room and watching their performance with and without a privacy filter around. The whole group was around 53% females and 47% males.

The men and women were given computers that had a privacy filter fitted to them. A privacy filter was thin screen on the side of the monitor that restricted who could see the screen. Subjects were given 10 minutes with the filter on and 10 minutes without the filter.

Monitored closely it was reported that women are far more productive, less likely to get distracted and when offered a chance to take a break, they are less likely to take it before they finish what they are doing.

Interestingly, for men, it was reported that men are actually less productive when there is a woman around, more prone to distractions and also more likely to take frequent breaks as well.

Working Flexible Hours Increase Productivity in Women

Often times, women have to work around their schedules at home or for their studies and kids. Whatever the reason may be, female freelancers are a lot more common than male freelancers.

Even when businesses offer their female employees part time employment, there's no way of knowing if that improves productivity or not.

Luckily, the EY and Chief Executive Women report can shed some light on it. With flexible hours, women are more productive, waste little to no time and are also able to deliver.

Furthermore, among 42.2% of any workforce work part-time or flexibly and the productivity of an organization is definitely significantly impacted on. Unfortunately, working part-time often means lower pay so it is about time that businesses start to recognize the amount of productivity they contribute towards their organization.

Businesses with Women Do Better

Every business knows that a diverse workforce is better and improves productivity. A diverse work force is the breeding ground for better ideas. Luckily, many businesses have started to take this fact seriously to heart.

Nonetheless, the Anita Borg Institute for Women and Technology took the time to conduct a study and publish a paper called '*The Case for Investing in Women*' which covered this topic intensively.

The presence of women in the workforce can drastically improve the overall productivity of the business. Among the many examples that the study gave, the following are the most notable points:

> When companies that rank in the Fortune 500 have female directors, the productivity of the organization went up increasing

the returns on capital investments to 66%, sales went up by 42% and increase on equity went up by 53%.

Studies that span over 17 countries showcase that among the various business industries, businesses that have more women in their workforce showcase more group efficiency, better psychological safety and more team confidence as well.

More diversity entails more creativity and more creativity increases the overall productivity.

Women happen to be one of the main driving forces behind creativity and diversity and with those two aspects, productivity is not far behind.

Now if you want to find out how you can become more productive as a part of your workforce, the next chapter will definitely help you find the answers to that.

IMPROVING WOMEN'S PRODUCTIVITY – LEARNING THE TRICKS OF THE TRADE

Now that we have looked at everything from a scientific point of view, it's time to be more practical and learn how to be productive in your work. The best thing about these tips is that you can use them whether you are at work or at your home, their results will definitely be visible.

Do the Hardest Task of the Day First

Don't shy away from the hard tasks. Oftentimes, the thought of conquering something hard can make people want to avoid that task. However, all you have to do is ask yourself *'What's the worst that can happen?'* Don't be afraid of making mistakes. That's the only way you can learn from them.

Don't be Afraid to Seek Help

When you have to start something, you may be afraid of doing the wrong thing. If you are uncertain about your skills, then go ahead and ask someone who knows how to accomplish the task.

Delegate Your Work

If you are working in a team, be sure to play up to its strengths and assign work to people on the basis of who can get what done as quickly as possible.

Eliminate Distractions

Put your phone on silent, don't log on to Facebook and do not open up different websites. Focus completely on your work and get some done before you even think about taking a break.

Reward Yourself

Use Facebook and your favorite website as a treat for yourself to indulge in during your break. This will eventually allow you to become more focused in your work.

Take Notes all the Time

Whether you are at work or at home, keep a pen and notepad near you. This way, you can easily jot down any important points relating to your task.

Make a Checklist

Moreover, you can make a checklist with which you can easily tick off all the tasks that you have done and all the tasks that are left. You can also scribble down any ideas that come to you that could be incorporated into your assignment.

PRODUCTIVITY SECRETS FROM ACCOMPLISHED WOMEN

All this stuff about productivity is bound to make you more curious and find out more about what the women who are in high positions in large firms. The following are some of the tips that they had to share with us:

Make Time for Down Time

It's important to have some down time in which you can relax. Moreover, at work, you can often close your cubicle or go out to the library or some other quiet place to organize your thoughts, relax and figure out some problems. Not making room for down time simply introduces a lot of stress in the day and a stressed mind is not a productive mind.

Take the Bull By the Horns

Don't let your problems fester and do not be afraid to resolve any problems that you might be facing. Oftentimes, it can be rather overwhelming and like feeling a box of dynamite explode when these problems finally burst out. Don't wait for that eruption to happen. Deal with the problem quickly and in a timely manner.

Don't Multi-Task

Multi-tasking, while encouraged, can become something that seriously hampers your productivity. Like a greedy kid who wants to keep all the candies for himself, you will end up with all the resources but get none of the work done.

The best thing to do in such situations is to learn to delegate your tasks. Follow up with the people you assign the tasks to, help clear out any difficulties that they might have and ask for updates. Then leave that task alone and work on the ones that require your immediate attention.

Cut Down on Social Media

While social media opened up a whole new world through which you can connect and promote your business, it is also a whole new world of distractions. Try to limit your social media time and make sure that you only use it during your break or at home if you want to. If your break gets longer because you lose track of time, then allot yourself 10 to 20 minutes and make sure you stick to it.

Giving the Right Environment

Make your workplace as comfortable for you as you possibly can. Place a few plants around your desk, pin up inspirational notes and make sure that you have a cushion or two on your chair that can make it comfortable for you. With all these elements and more making your workplace more pleasant, you will be able to relax and focus more on your work at hand.

Whether you apply these tried and tested tips and tricks at home or at work, you will be sure to get plenty of results from them.

CONCLUSION

So we come to end of our eBook, dear readers, and all I can say is that I hope that this eBook has been informative in helping you understand the importance of productivity, the role it plays in our life and how it relates to women in general.

Many times you may find yourself bogged down in situations where you have three or more tasks to accomplish and still have to go home and do cooking and cleaning chores. With the help of this eBook, you can easily make such a hectic life easier for yourself and learn to find some respite in your everyday life.

And if anyone tries to tell you that you aren't productive, just shove this eBook into their face and we'll teach them a thing or too. For now, we bid you adieu and hope to meet again in some other eBook.

www.ingramcontent.com/pod-product-compliance
Lightning Source LLC
Chambersburg PA
CBHW072049190526
45165CB00019B/2249